Bringing it all home

Hélène's property searches

Hélène Ferrari

From original book « Gagner ses pénates »

Hélène Ferrari

Translate from French by Lynne Logan

Coverbook – 2016©Hélène Ferrari
From a original illustration of Charlotte du Jour

ISBN : 978-2-9556411-2-5

Foreword

Why write a collection of short stories centred around real estate ? Because there's a strong connection between the home and the self. What I mean is that the home is a reflection of the soul. It's where we 'abide', where we forge connections and affirm our values. Also and above all, the home is where we belong, our frame of reference, our roots, our relationship with the soil and with the world. I'm something of an ecologist and that applies equally to interiors. In the words of the philosopher, we must each cultivate our own garden.

To cultivate is to grow. We often forget that the grower must first sow and only then can they evolve. Rather like an entrepreneur, in fact. Entrepreneurship is an adventure. Mine consists of facilitating meaningful exchanges, of connecting those on a quest for their origins with those who are passing on the fruits of a moment lived.

Bringing together life-changers and treasure-hunters is wonderful work. It's about trading in dreams and realities. Dreams are the stuff of possibilities – and of the senses. Reality is earthbound but I'm at ease there because, you see, I'm not just a broker, I'm like the falconer who casts his eyes upwards to see the beauty of the world. In my work I need my feet on the ground and my soul in the air. Insight must not just be rational but instinctive because, to search for a home, you need to start by discovering what makes you unique. Treasure exists only in as much as we can see it sparkle. I wanted to write about that.

The dovecot

I'll call him Olivier. He's a French TV personality. This multi-talented individual has several strings to his bow but let's say he's a writer. In fact, when he comes to see me that morning, it's because he's looking for a place where he can write in peace away from the hustle and bustle, a temple to creativity. He's not sure exactly what he wants and there lies the difficulty. Unformed thoughts are hard to express. He figured that by getting in touch with a professional he would be offered help and advice. Alas, no! He's really on his high horse now and, all things considered, I would never have imagined our Mr Olivier quite so scathing. Once bitten, twice shy. He just doesn't like estate agents. A friend who was trying to help suggested he come to see me. This is the final push, he says. He's tired of being given the run around. I tell him to stay right there and I'll fetch him a coffee. Should I make it a decaf? "Okay, I'll play ball," he quips. So a picker-up it is. What else?

The location doesn't really matter, although it should be as remote as possible, but still five minutes from all amenities. He doesn't like driving. When I'm behind the wheel I get a real sense of freedom; there's nothing new in that. But for him, it's the height of boredom and practically constitutes torture. He sees that I'm sympathetic to his plight and continues in softer tones and with a faint smile. No, it's a high-speed train station that he needs, with a direct link to the capital and his Parisian apartment, for the sake of his work. If it wasn't for that, he would have taken himself off to some kind of retreat long ago... It needs to be a direct link. "Because, you see, if it isn't I mess up". With professional, deadpan delivery he tells me that every single time he misses the connection. He's irritated by noise, finds chatter intolerable and overcrowding suffocating so he cuts himself off as much as possible, by way of protection, with headphones and a good book. And his mind wanders as he thinks, meditates, dreams or falls asleep to the extent that, by the time he snaps out of it, it's too late. "And", he says, incidentally, "I hate waiting. It's kind of hard on you but I'd rather warn you in advance". We've already saved time... He adds brusquely that all of this has to remain between us. By this he means that I don't know him, that I've never met him and that his property trials and tribulations must remain confidential. I reassure him; discretion comes as standard. And since we're sharing secrets, I ask him where in Paris he has his bachelor pad, clarifying straight off that I need to know on a purely professional basis so that I can focus my search around the nearest railway station.

I give him an idea of what to expect and how I operate and outline our respective roles. He's happy with that. The point of him coming here was precisely to keep his involvement to a bare minimum. Answering questions and talking about his feelings is what he does best, it's his thing. Well, that's fortunate because that's all he'll be doing. I ask him to tell me about his flat. Apparently it's a mess. He had hoped to find a soulmate to sort him out but that wasn't to be. Papers, books and pictures are the permanent features. A decent amount of light and a clear view from the window so that he can open up to the world. Add a few cosy touches for the sake of comfort and there you have it. A dash of authenticity is always welcome. What about the style? He laughs. He thinks he's pretty stylish... Of course he does, so do I, but is Olivier more François Mansartor Philippe Starck? He pauses a beat. "Both", he breathes. "Well, seventeenth-century, yes but now that you mention it, not Mansart". We chat a little longer; he's open-minded but, even so, we should avoid the baroque and anything too bourgeois or pretentious. The most important thing is the setting. We talk about art. At this point he asks if he's under police questioning but I finally get him to tell me what he likes. Again, he appreciates a wide variety of styles but especially colour, light, abstract and paintings which uplift and inspire. I do my fortune telling number to check I'm on the right track, something along the lines of, "For you I see the countryside with open spaces, a distant forest, remote but not too far from a village ; hilly but not overly so (that would be too rugged) and I'm sensing that the sea holds no attraction for you". He's happy with that.

Now here comes the science. I immerse myself in my anamorphic maps. What's that, I hear you say? It's simple. Anamorphosisis a distortion of space using a mathematical vector interpolation model based on actual data. For the more literary-minded among you, let's just say I have maps that distort in proportion to journey times, by train for example. I want to be kind to Olivier so I slightly increase the level of sunshine and draw a line between Rennes and Belfort. He'd stressed the importance of light (I appreciate there's an element of extrapolation here) but there's no need to panic; the process is reversible. I set the journey time at around two hours, which I think is a fair compromise for a busy man. Olivier's lifestyle offers flexibility in this respect. Why not cut it down to one hour, you say? Because at the mere mention of Compiègne, Rambouillet or Orléans, Olivier starts to feel like a commuter. What he wants is the greenery of Normandy without the rain. And, to be perfectly frank, we'd also talked numbers. During the science stage, you don't just deal in hours and kilometres; you deal mainly in Keuros - short for Kiloeuros. The higher the Keuros, the greater the spend. And Olivier is aiming high. During the week it's all about creating a timeless space ; at the weekend it's about friends, lots of friends. You convert square metres and hectares to Keuros and extract the featureless wasteland. I map out three search areas; the working hypotheses can be amended if necessary : Tours-Angers, a number of points between Poitiers and Angoulême and Montbard-Lyon. The first two options have rail links to Montparnasse and the third to the Gare de Lyon. "Going out west sounds great", was Olivier's reaction, "and, what's more, the weather's better". I promise to come up with an initial selection of properties very soon. He doesn't like to wait.

The same scene some time later. Olivier is sitting in the same armchair in the same position, left leg over the other, elbows dangling over the armrests and hands crossed in front of him. Not exactly open to the world. His chin is slightly drawn in and his gaze is directed towards the floor. The uppermost foot is tapping out a frantic rhythm. You'd think I was about to tell him the results of his blood tests. Close your eyes... breathe deeply, now open your eyes...and voila! The slideshow begins. The Loire Valley, an unusual eighteenth-century manor house, clean lines, large windows overlooking the parkland, hills in the distance. He places his feet on the floor, sits up straight and says, "Not bad at all!" I suggest we continue while the iron's hot. We can conduct the debriefing afterwards. The Indre Valley, an architect-designed house with a similar setting to the manor house. "Yes, it's got it all... except a soul..." That isn't me talking, it's him. I was expecting this but he had to feel it for himself. The Echelle Valley in the Charente - a rural hamlet which, seen from the exterior, could date from the eighteenth century. In fact, each new century has brought more and more home comforts while the oldest parts of the interior are medieval. Unsophisticated but harmonious, modest but comfortable, it has the added advantage of being colourful with its whitewashed stone and orange roof tiles conjuring up something of the south. Olivier remains silent but his mouth hangs slightly open. His jaw drops even further when, as the camera pans round, a light mist can be seen enveloping the wooded valleys. The film is almost over. I break the silence to mention that the nearby buildings can accommodate occasional guests with a corresponding reduction in the annual charges. And then there's the dovecote, the ivory tower par excellence, a celebration of nature. "So when can I see it?"

In the shadow of the Father

Before making a start on the tomato salad, I listen carefully as Dominique and Sylvie quickly run through the terms of my mission. They're among the best friends of a couple of my clients. The tomatoes, glistening with olive oil and aromatic herbs from the garden, can wait. Dominique has just retired and at the age of 62 has no intention of putting his dreams and plans on hold. Quite the contrary. He runs a hand through his perfectly-styled hair as he tries to find the right words. Always well-groomed, his signet ring with its beautiful coat of arms reflects the Provence sun. My clients in Bordeaux had already described him to me: he does indeed cut a fine figure. He's careful in his choice of words. He must choose them as he does his objets d'art and antiques, for their symbolism and their beauty. A lover of history and heritage, Dominique is a collector. He loves beautiful things and takes special care to show them at their best. Even so, his life is far from being limited to memories and display cases. Would you believe he's also an Aikido master? Sylvie, with great fondness for her gallant partner, adds that he's also a DIY enthusiast. I want to hear more. They tell me they like their home to have a certain elegance. I wasn't expecting to hear this. In truth, I had no preconceptions at all. I listen, I sense and I add the colours to my virtual palette. By happy chance, I'm drowning in Sylvie's electric blue eyes where the waves are breaking in a rough sea... We're not very far from the water. You can't smell the sea from here but there's a wind that feels as if the coast is snaking along behind the plane trees in the town square. Sylvie was a catamaran champion in her youth, so water is never very far away. Water, wind and the swell of the sea... Best be careful not to tread on her toes.

The couple spend their summers in sunny Provence. We're going to visit their summer residence after the fig tart. The "traditional Provencal farmhouse" is actually a new build. I could have been disappointed but I'm not... what a view! The terrace overlooks the Sainte Croix lake. The view is magnificent. The water matches the colour of Sylvie's eyes. The lake is calm. Sailboats glide along in the distance behind the pedalos in the foreground. Beyond that, the steep rocks of the Verdon Gorges. The view is soothing and breathtaking at the same time; you'd never get tired of admiring it. Now I'm even more curious to see their Paris flat where they take refuge in winter.

I question them to get a better understanding of what they're looking for. They each reveal what's important to them, as much by what they say as by what they don't. So Dominique and Sylvie are looking for a character property, perhaps in Brittany but nothing is set in stone. They'll need to sell their "Provencal farmhouse" before buying a new property. They're endearing and full of contrasts and contradictions that I'll have to take into account. One idea bursts forth just to be swept away by another a minute later. It's not easy to sum up what they're looking for and match it with the realities of the market. They seem to understand that compromises may have to be made, but still it's not clear. I need to listen to their dreams and try to understand them without saying a word. In any case they're about as flexible as two tightly-strung wires. The "details" don't change their point of view : executive management positions, no children... I create a diversion and we continue with their story. I want to understand where they're coming from so that I can visualise where they're going.

Dominique and Sylvie have been spending the summer in Provence for many years. They love to relax in the sun, sipping a little rosé wine under the plane trees in a charming village with the fountain gurgling softly nearby. "They've been coming to the village for so long that they're almost one of us," said the innkeeper as he brought the tapenade to the table. Dominique, the artistic DIYer and Sylvie, the amazing lady of the house, have managed to transform their

1990's architect-designed house into an attractive, elegant and welcoming farmhouse. Plush sofas by the fireplace, a bistro-style table under the cool arches of the sunny patio, deck chairs on the terrace, all combining to create absolute perfection. White all over with a profusion of flowers and a swimming pool overlooking the lake and scrubland, their house is a real must-have in Pagnol country. Imagine my surprise when they ask me to find them a home... in Brittany. No more hot days or tomatoes and olives from the garden, goodbye to aioli and rosemary, Norman roof tiles and oleander. Hello granite and sea spray... not to mention crepes, cider, shellfish and hydrangeas. It's not that I have anything against Brittany. I spent my childhood summers there. I love it and still go there regularly.

I had to get things clear in my head. I dangle some bait, and get a bite! The upkeep of the house is challenging... the tourists are noisy with their hordes of kids... all summer there are motorhomes crawling up and down the narrow, winding road to the lake... I seem almost to have angered them now. But it's still not enough for me. Why Brittany? What has it got to offer them? Dominique and Sylvie really feel the need to breathe clean air, to leave behind the sweltering heat of Provence, the mistral wind that drives you mad and sweeps away everything in its path. This is a major development: the idea of pleasure is giving way to the need for security. And basking in the sun becomes futile. In Paris, they watch the sparrows on their balcony. Some country-dwelling friends have the nice idea of hanging bird food from the tree branches. Quietly watching the birds in the little garden is relaxing. And the noise has become unbearable. The need for (inner?) peace and quiet seems to be essential. What they want now is to live simply, to get to know interesting people, without, or almost without, value judgments, to stop hoisting the sails and put down anchor.

The idea of Brittany is mainly Sylvie's. The Sainte Croix lake is calm. The reflection on the water is no longer one of youth. Her catamaran may have been replaced by a motorboat but the gentle ripples are lacking in sea air and vitality. On balance, I think I understand that Dominique and Sylvie now want to live somewhere meaningful, a place set in its own time, in history, in the life they were sadly unable to give.

I present them with some ideas and their answers confirm what I had thought. In actual fact, what matters is neither the location nor the number of square meters nor the design. What matters is to meet a deep yearning, a yearning that is perhaps even a little spiritual. One word seemed appropriate: a "home". I had to find a quiet, safe place where Dominique could go about his business and live in peace with his beloved. A place where Sylvie could contemplate her wild memories. A safe and secure place where nothing is pre-determined, where they can mark their time on earth, a place where they'll no longer just be retired executives but can be themselves. And, fundamentally, where they can be valued simply for who they are.

A few proposals and viewing reports later, I sense that the shock of uprooting will be really hard for them: the properties are too austere, too suburban or too far north (in northern Brittany), poor value for money in southern Brittany and so on. In fact, they're not really ready to give up the sun. There's a bare minimum requirement in terms of warmth and colour. I make an alternative suggestion: the northern part of the southwest: Charente. The Atlantic climate is mild and sunny with blue skies and much lower humidity. The summers are dry and warm, but not excessively so. Not much wind and not many tourists away from the coast. Norman churches and proper homes. Although, admittedly, it's around an hour's drive to the sea, I think I'm onto something and I tell them what I'm thinking. They go for it! The proximity of the TGV to Paris in a good two hours, the benefits of the climate and the beauty of the architecture are all bonuses for them. I switch on my computer and show them my photos. The beauty of the contrasting red roof tiles against the slate is incomparable, striking and undeniable and it doesn't take a genius to see it. In the course of our discussions, we become interested in the Boisné way, a Roman road south of Cognac between Saintes and Périgueux. This ancient route makes an appearance at just the right time. It's marked on the Roman Peutinger map. No "traditional farmhouses" here. Instead they have manor houses or chateaux but the feeling of being close to the land and the sense of history are still there. The attractive prices making for a good deal are the icing on the cake, or rather the grapes in the Pineau!

So I'm off on my search again. I need to gather information on the ground, talk to the locals, assess the location, meet some homeowners, view some properties, soak up the atmosphere of the places I visit and feel the soul of the houses. I view character properties and magical places which all have at least one downside: too windswept, heavy infrastructure, environmental pollution or planned works giving cause for concern. There are lots of tragic stories too and I'm sad to hear of houses being ruined by poor restoration. The damage done to them would offend Dominique's aesthetic sensibilities and Sylvie's search for authenticity. I confess to feeling somewhat disheartened...

While exploring an unfamiliar valley, I come across something unexpected; I find myself in front of a beautiful medieval house, a little austere, admittedly, but so very intriguing with its mullioned windows and Norman doors. It's got real character and an unspoilt setting; it's a reasonable size and has a small enclosed garden overlooking the village with a lovely view. It's uninhabited and renovation work is urgently needed. It holds my attention, and soon Dominique and Sylvie's, for several weeks. They follow my investigations and the twists and turns of the story like addicts of a television series. They want to see it in spite of the downsides I've told them about. In the heart of the village, a square, eleventh-century tower provides access to the entrance towards the spiral stone staircase serving each storey. A charming corridor leads to the other side of the building and the spacious living room with a cobbled floor of sandstone and gravel dotted with pebbles, then onto an enclosed terrace forming a small patio, protected by a lovely carved wooden balcony. Unfortunately, the main room is rather dark, as is the case in most medieval houses and knocking down original walls which are two meters thick is not an option. The terraced garden is barely usable and will need a lot of maintenance with very little return. As for the house, it faces partly onto the street, a small quiet street admittedly but net curtains will be needed at the windows. The most disappointing thing, however, is how much the sellers have neglected their treasure... the roof is in serious disrepair and water is seeping into the beams and walls inside the medieval house. The sense of neglect is unbearable for Dominique and Sylvie, given its (and their) history.

They don't know it yet but a solicitor has already told me about a similar property for sale. He doesn't have the brochure but suggests I take a look. I'm delighted to discover a very beautiful building barely visible from the street on the church square of a charming village. We are fifteen minutes from the previous town. I don't learn much from my visit. It's obviously a Norman priory. I can see beautiful mullioned windows and a few arrow slits. The size seems ideal, the walled garden is quiet and the authentic building in good condition. The rest is invisible to the eye but, to quote the Little Prince, is visible to the heart. The search for the owners is intense and exciting. It takes several weeks. Telephone messages, visits to the house, notes in the letterbox and information from the town hall. Finally the owners call me. Their tone is polite but rather cool. It's only after my first lengthy and productive visit that trust is well and truly established. My hosts are absolutely charming and in love with their beautiful house. I sense I may have found the ideal home...

The priory dates from the twelfth century but historical data is scarce before the fifteenth century. It is known that the monks took up residence in the monastery in 1407 which was at the time three times its current size. The living area which remains today is very attractive and, unexpectedly, very well suited to modern needs. It's a huge house which was refashioned during the Renaissance. There are large mullioned windows to the south with wide porches to the north. These now form bay windows which look out over the garden and the church whose stonework, gilded by the sun, lights up the house like a mirror. The full-length rooms and high windows let in lots of light in spite of the thick walls, that distinctive amber light which is a feature of the region. Even if the stair turret is long gone, the building, constructed in the twelfth century from limestone mined in local quarries and its square tower and numerous outbuildings, still stands proud. Finally, the interior restoration has been carried out sympathetically, while retaining the beautiful original features, making the most of this huge and determinedly contemporary priory. The garden doesn't disappoint either. It circles the house to take advantage of the warmth from the south and the coolness from the north. Between the church and the priory, a peaceful English garden lit by the stone of the church and totally private thanks to its high walls, offers a real haven of peace. It's a place where you're perfectly safe, out of sight of everyone, except perhaps the Good Lord himself. The blue tits are pecking at the bird food hanging from the blackberry bush in the shade of the fig tree. There's not a sound, not a breath, just the rustling of the pages of the history book which Dominique is devouring, an elbow resting on the garden table like a king on his throne. Running his hand through his hair, the lord of the manor is putting down his roots while his wife, Sylvie, anchors her azure gaze in the Charente skies. My mission is accomplished.

A buccaneer at heart

"Deep in the Gulf of Artaban, with Bago on the horizon, a cry rings out from the crow's nest. Three English ships swept along by the north wind. Surcouf recognizes the brig, Ganges, then two Bengal vessels doubtless loaded with rice. The brig fires a warning shot forcing us to show their colours. Surcouf imagines how welcome such a cargo would be on the Ile de France where famine was threatening. "The Ile de France is Mauritius now," explained his father. "Surcouf has no letter of marque so, legally, he can't attack. But his buccaneering spirit prevails. He hesitates not one second before hoisting the tricolor. He gives the order to open fire. The ships lower their colours and surrender. Night is already falling and the pontoons are bedecked with lights to guide the sailors. Watched from the deck of the three-master, the English ships tremble for a moment atop the waves before sinking into the sea. Goodnight, Titouan."

Young Titouan's adventures began outside a house on the fringes of Saint-Malo with a retaliatory mission against the Keriant brothers whom he pelted with stones before returning home with bloody knees. It was the same scenario every time and his father said that thugs like him ended up in jail. It's not only thugs who end up in jail, thought Titouan, and the deserving ones don't stay there long. Hadn't Jean Bart and Forbin escaped from Plymouth in 1689? Titouan's ancestors must have been among the crowds who thronged the docks and city walls to greet them. The news had preceded them thanks to a fisherman who had passed them in their boat north of

Cap Fréhel. The two privateers had reached Erquy after fifty hours of rowing and continued on foot from Dinard. It was a triumphant homecoming.

Today Titouan lives in Paris, a creative computer programmer who worked hard and took evening classes to help him set up his video games business. Emulating the great American dream, the company was bought over by a high-powered group and Titouan was able to grow his projects, investments, successes and conquests. It was a busy man who called me that day: "I'd like to buy a nice house in Brittany. Would you be able to find me one?" he says, getting straight to the point. We briefly discuss what he's looking for, I explain my method and we meet at his office near Montparnasse, the traditional Breton quarter of Paris. The walls are covered with old leaflets, historical engravings and other story book-style images, all from Saint-Malo. I go to take a closer look at an old framed document: "On the *Grenedan*, he is already showing great aplomb. The privateer frigate, with twenty-eight guns and two hundred crewmen, has already taken over *the Guillaume*, an English sailing ship loaded with sugar, indigo, cotton and copper, an English ketch, *the Providence*, with forked masts resembling a yacht and a Dutch three-master, *the Saint-Jacques,* with twenty-six guns, which he took with the sword.""It's a first edition from1773," declares Titouan, suddenly appearing from nowhere. "Duguay-Trouin, a hundred years after his birth...," he continues before inviting me to take a seat and telling me about his plans. It's easy to see why he wants to buy a holiday home full of character and history near Saint-Malo. But before I have the chance to ask him for more details, we're off exploring Canada with Jacques Cartier. Back then, privateers were harassing enemy merchant and military ships. These gentlemen of Saint-Malo returned from the Indies loaded with sweet oriental perfumes, silks, tobacco, porcelain and spices and sailed the seven seas from New found land to Pondicherry, from China to the Americas. I finally manage to interrupt the flow. "A *malouinière?*" I venture, referring to the typical manor houses built in Saint-Malo by ship owners and privateers in the 18th century. For a long time he stares into space, saying nothing. Then he turns his gaze towards me. "There aren't any!" he sighs.

For me it was an emotional journey back into my own past, when, as a child and then a teenager, I stayed there during the holidays with memories of feasting on delicious crepes. The *malouinières* were in vogue between 1650 and 1730. Saint-Malo was becoming congested so they were built further inland all the way across the peninsula to Cancale, otherwise known as the "Clos-Poulet", a corruption of "Pou Alet" Alet country, Alet being the old Gallo-Roman town on the site of what is now Saint-Servant. The location was strategic with the town's fortifications providing ship owners and privateers with protection from English incursions and also helping them avoid the royal tax collectors. Ships returning from the Orient were quietly diverted towards isolated coves where their precious cargo was unloaded under cover of darkness. The *malouinière* has an almost military feel to it. They often bear the hallmarks of the king's engineers such as Garangeau, a pupil of Vauban. Their architecture is austere and well-proportioned. The central section, generally built of granite from the island of Chausey, is roughcast and their tapered roofs and chimneys can be seen from afar. Until the 17th century, the windows were designed for the needs of the time but by the 18th century they had become symmetrical and regular. For all that, the *malouinières* are not lacking in sophistication with their wooden car vings and French gardens testifying to the bygone splendor of the buccaneering town.

Even at that time there were many rich town-dwellers who wanted to settle in tranquil Saint-Malo but few actually succeeded. Today there are only 112 *malouinières* making it a niche market, almost a family market, and opportunities to buy are few and short-lived. The difficulty lies in knowing how to approach the owners of your perfect hideaway. That was Titouan's problem. Perhaps because the *malouinière* and its owner form a couple with entwined personalities. They are both imposing with their mathematical precision and their delightful combination of granite austerity and the warm classicism of ornamental shrubs. Writing in his blog about the Breton character in general, Stéphane notes: "In this distant land, this peninsula clinging onto the Eurasian continent, the environment has shaped both the culture and the character of its inhabitants. Whether life was land-based or required sea legs, it was hard, and even downright brutal on occasions. Try growing crops on a granitic soil that's acidic, poor quality and water logged." There's nothing on the internet about the character of *malouinière* owners in particular, probably because it's always the captain who decides when, or if, to show his colours. But it would be unthinkable for Titouan the conqueror, Titouan the rebel, Titouan the non-conformist to submit to the mercy of the waves.

I drop the working anchor at Clos Poulet, pull in the ropes and cast off towards familiar territory. Some residents have chosen a more modern lifestyle and decided to part with the costly family estate. Others are bravely working to make the most of their heritage. But all of them take the time to reminisce and each one of their memories opens up a path for me to explore.

Today's host welcomes me with a manly handshake. The lady of the house is waiting for us in the drawing room with an iced tea. It's hot in Brittany this summer. I'm invited to take a seat in a comfortable armchair hand-embroidered by a famous ancestor. The countess, whose delicate hands are perfectly manicured, recounts what has become of our shared acquaintances and the *malouinières* in the area. She explains the oval shape of the drawing room, inspired by the chateau of Champs-sur-Marne. Its architect, Bullet de Chamblain, might also be the designer of this house but it's uncertain as the builder's archives are stored away at the Swedish court where he worked after leaving France. Because of this there are no plans available for many of the *malouinières*. The count speaks bluntly, leaving little to the imagination. He is proud to show me around his home. The visit begins, as is the custom, at the grand entrance to admire the classical harmony of the north facade. This is topped by a triangular pediment dating from 1707 whose coat of arms was sadly destroyed during the revolution. The south facade has a central, semi-circular section also topped by a triangular tympanum decorated with allegories illustrating the exploits of the family's great seafaring ancestor. From its sixteen windows, you can admire the French garden with its flowerbeds of hydrangeas and rhododendrons. I am examining the Louis XVI wooden garlands framing a Carrara marble fireplace, probably brought from a nearby castle during restoration, when the countess who has now joined us calls over tome :

- Do you know the Ps?
- No, not personally.
- That's a pity. It would probably be good for you to meet them.
- Do you think so?
- Most certainly. They want to sell their property...

I am introduced by the countess and welcomed by the Ps with the same slightly aloof politeness. The children are at the beach with their own little ones. They'll be back late in the afternoon so we have time to view the property. Marie-Claire shows me round the garden of about 2 hectares with a beautiful, unobstructed view of the river Rance... a rare and totally unspoiled setting. The French garden had been rather neglected but the flowerbeds are still well defined and the box hedge doesn't seem to have been affected by the snout moth which had done so much damage this summer. Simple but harmonious outbuildings are set back slightly so there's a lovely view of the house from the driveway. The property, a true cousin of the one belonging to my matchmaker, is made up of three interlinking sections. The center sits slightly forward with the two wings behind. The building as a whole is beautifully proportioned with triangular pediments with granite fittings on each section. It was a lavish and beautifully-maintained rose hedge that would change the formal tone of the viewing. I love flowers and the soft pink reflection on the granite, strangely reminiscent of the flower itself, was simply beautiful. We pick a few stems together and take them back to the office. Our shared love of nature had broken the ice.

With its exceptional location, its 300^{m2} and usable outbuildings, the *malouinière* has the potential to meet all of Titouan's needs and desires. All that's missing is the dovecot he had dreamed of. However, there is one major drawback : it needs a lot of work. I activate my mental arithmetic function. The electrics, heating, drains, sanitation and window frames all need to be replaced. Bathrooms would need to be installed. The wallpaper is seriously dated and the paint is flaking. But the essentials are sound. The roof seems to be in good condition and, very importantly, the house doesn't seem to be damp. There's absolutely no sign of any salt deposits. On this hot summer's day, I attribute the cool interior to the thick walls. Feeling the cold as I do, even in summer, I would have instantly noticed any sign of dampness. The kitchen, in its original condition, is a warm, pleasant space due to its size and the large, welcoming fireplace with its memories of many a family gathering; it should be a winner. So, overall, this is a very nice holiday home but definitely not a comfortable main residence.

We haven't yet talked about finances but I obviously have a price range in mind. Marie-Claire is the sole owner which is why she wants to sell. She can't look after the house and prefers the comfort of her Paris flat. If necessary, next year she'll rent a large house to accommodate her young mariners and their parents. I try to get an idea of her expectations but she says she needs to talk to the rest of the family. Two days later they name a price, one that I consider too high given the amount of work to be done. I tell them so but there's no way they're going to change their mind for now. But time often works its magic so I focus on preparing the property schedule for the impatient Titouan.

In fact, he's worried. "It's beautiful, it's chic and it's classy". So he likes it! It's true that it's exactly what he's looking for but there's the renovation work to consider. He spends a long time reading and re-reading my estimates. I can see the numbers racing at full speed through his mind, working out how he can buy this beautiful *malouinière* before he's even seen it.

The viewing is arranged. We meet there one Saturday in September. It's still mild and the late afternoon sun casts a golden glow on the west facade. The leaves on the trees are beginning to turn red, with their shadows on the yew beds making the driveway seem even grander. Not much is said during the viewing and it's not clear whether Titouan is imagining swash buckling adventures of old or weighing up how much this house could mean to him. He takes me to one side and throws down the challenge: "You've found my *malouinière*. Now I need you to negotiate the price!"

Epilogue: The negotiations were tough and would continue all through the autumn but the captain will be hoisting his colours on December 24th. Nedeleg Laouen! Merry Christmas!

Double or quits

This is the story of how a fairly typical property search turned into something resembling a television series. But this isn't fiction; this is reality. The adventure begins when Agnès and Philippe welcome me into their beautiful apartment in the Gambetta district of Paris. My hosts are charming, open and inquiring. In this bright room where the white walls illuminate the russet shades of the furniture, they ask me about my business, my method and what I'm currently working on. The conversation is productive and, even though the subjects are practical, the questions run deep. They quickly grasp how I operate and how I can help them with their search for a new property. You can feel a sort of energy and transparency in this home where all kinds of ideas come together and where light and space abound. But the outlook is restricted by the neighbouring buildings. Through the large windows, I can see plane trees between the balconies but the zinc roof tops are obstructing the view. There's a more open vista on the other side overlooking the Père Lachaise cemetery but from this angle it's very much a cityscape. I ask them about their plans. They want to move out to the country. They need depth of field even if they don't actually want to toil in them. I talk about the Parisian lifestyle : shopping, shows, transport and so on. Their careers are demanding. They need space and relaxation without being completely isolated. Agnès wants to be less than 30 minutes from the capital at off-peak times. She works mainly from home and is free to manage her own schedule. Philippe's work means he flies out of Roissy several times a week. "But not the suburbs," they tell me straight away. "We're leaving

Paris to get a change of air."But there are suburbs and suburbs...
"We called you because we're looking for a character property in a
peaceful location!" they add with a smile. It's true that this is my
core business. They stress the need for space, for themselves and
their guests. They have a lot of visitors at the weekends. If they're
far from Paris the house will have to be able to accommodate their
children and friends. As I listen to them, I immediately think of a
manor house that I had been told was up for sale the month before : a
sophisticated property with open spaces, a stylish place with wooded
coverts and a few fields, not far from the motorway and with guest
rooms. It might just fit the bill but I still needed to find out where It
is and arrange a viewing. I plan to carry out my investigations and
prepare my reports in the first week of January, if at all possible. The
week after the festive period is usually fairly quiet. So here I am,
well wrapped up from head to toe, exploring the south of the Oise
region. Access to Paris is easy by public transport and Charles de
Gaulle Airport is nearby. This leafy, crescent-shaped area is the
perfect target for my search. I know it well; I've got good contacts
here and a manor house to find.

I really do love property hunting in winter. It's fun to spot houses
which are usually hidden by foliage peeping through the bare trees.
Unfortunately, the wintry weather has no effect on the thorns of the
black locust trees and I get pricked in my attempts to satisfy my
curiosity. A weak Epiphany sun is shining as I take a turn along a
bridle path to see the manor house appear to me between two large
oak trees, a revelation indeed. The house is L-shaped. The whole
structure evokes the eighteenth century and is of immaculate
construction. However, the boundary wall and the grand entrance
hide much of the facade. The location and size of the property and
the setting are ideal but I can't see any further than that. It's 4
o'clock and the sun is already beginning to set. As I retrace my
steps, I start to prepare the approach I'll adopt the next day when I
phone the owners to try to get a quick appointment. Back at my
office in Chantilly, I review all the properties I've seen that day. I
sort through my photographs and keep coming back to the wonderful
manor house which had made such an impression on me. I need to
view it as quickly as possible. I'll have to be at my most persuasive.

On the boundary wall of the estate, a beautiful old brass bell already reflects the spirit of the place. No video intercom here, just a pull on a lovely little chain to let them know I've arrived. The big reygate opens instantly and a beautiful, tall, dark-haired woman signals for me to join her in the courtyard. My slow progress up the driveway gives me an opportunity to look around. The eighteenth-century buildings appear to have been reworked. There's a main building and a wing set further back. They were probably originally separate but had been joined together in the last century. Giulia welcomes me warmly and invites me to follow her inside. Draped in a pastel-coloured shawl, she doesn't seem to feel the cold and gives me a few moments to admire the facades. I'll take another look later but I can't help but marvel at the proportions. The main section of the house is on two levels and has six rows of windows. A moulded balcony runs be neath the first storey windows. I don't want to keep her waiting any longer; we go inside. The main door of the house is topped by a low arch and decorated with two simple pilasters reaching up to the balcony. The more recent building, constructed at right angles, hasn't been renovated but serves to protect the pleasant, paved courtyard with its two-hundred-year-old lime tree.

Giulia offers me coffee while we wait for her husband to join us. Jean-Luc, who has the complexion of a man used to working outdoors, takes a seat at the large dining-room table. Giulia has regular dinner parties there; they clearly enjoy socialising and sharing. They tell me about their business. They'd like to expand, further south... they have some very interesting leads. Their eyes sparkle at the mention of their initial explorations. They return to the theme of their bed and breakfast business. We compare our professional passions, our ambitions and our concept of service. They tell me more about the people they've met. They need these constant visitors. In fact, they're expecting two couples that evening. They have two suites booked for a christening to be held the following day at the cathedral in Senlis. This property really is perfect for guests. Each of the five bedrooms has its own bathroom and there are numerous living rooms : a sitting room, billiard room, smoking room and a reception room in the adjoining barn which is hired out for weddings. The rooms are laid out almost in a straight line and are spacious and bright in spite of the season, with rural views stretching far into the distance. The number of guests it can accommodate also meets my specifications. I really think Agnès and Philippe will be taken with this manor. I'm hoping it will be love at first sight.

A viewing is quickly arranged for them, so impatient are they are to see the gem they've been coveting since I sent them the property report. It has to be said that Giulia is not only a wonderful hostess but she also has a real talent for decorating her manor. Everything that passes through her hands is a joy to behold. My photographs have made the most of her talents. It's not surprising that Agnès and Philippe are enthralled by the charm of this country seat. At the viewing, the questions continue non-stop for four hours. The joy and wonder can be seen on their faces as they pass through each door way. They love the property. They book a suite for the following weekend under the pretext of testing out the journey time to Paris. The formal offer arrives on my desk barely two weeks after the first viewing. The financing terms are ideal and the price being offered is fair. If there's any negotiation to be done, I think it will be on time scales. I'm confident and pleased with the near completion of this smoothly-handled assignment which is going to suit everyone down to the ground.

The traffic is heavy which annoys me as I'm keen to announce the good news to the vendors. They're already waiting for me at the door and I sense that Giulia and Jean-Luc are nervous. Moving house is of course a major life event but now, with real embarrassment, seated side by side at the normally welcoming table, they shake their heads in unison. "No, it's just not possible," they protest. They're quite simply refusing to sell. I almost fall off my chair. They're worried about their plans not being sufficiently advanced and are imagining themselves out on the street. I reassure them. There are several ways to resolve the issue, it's a common problem and the buyers are flexible on timescales. It's no use. In fact, I now realize they haven't yet found their "love-at-first-sight" property. Of course I tell them that finding "love-at-first-sight" properties is what I do best.

We move on to season 2. So I now have a new assignment, for Giulia and Jean-Luc this time. They hadn't really made the leap into the future even though they had already visited numerous properties for sale in south-west France. Some of them had been the stuff of dreams but, without having sold their manor house, the purchase was put on hold each time and they lost out on the opportunity. It's par for the course really. With this offer, I've backed them into a corner. By taking up this golden opportunity, they can finally live their dream. I'm rushing them but they trust me and give me the go-ahead to carry out their search : a chateau in the Périgord or Gironde region which would allow them to increase their guest capacity. Jean-Luc, weary of his consultancy work, could take early retirement and join his wife in managing the guesthouse. There's something in it for Giulia too as she wants her two daughters and three grandchildren to able to stay with them on a regular basis.

I haven't forgotten about my Parisian couple. I'm sorry for the frustration caused by this situation and I appreciate how reasonably they react. "Never mind, we can wait till you find them the ideal chateau. You found one for us, you'll find one for them," jokes Philippe. I admire his way of thinking and am flattered by their confidence and but what a challenge for me! How long will it take me to find the chateau of their dreams? And will Agnès and Philippe wait?

The pressure is mounting and I end up shutting myself away in my office to give the search my full attention. It's all about working efficiently : identifying search areas, feeding back information, compiling files on target properties, carrying out searches on the ground and, finally, writing up reports for Giulia and Jean-Luc while keeping in touch with Agnès and Philippe. Both couples must remain fully committed as their fates are now inextricably linked.

In mid-April, about two months after Giulia and Jean-Luc had signed the letter of engagement, a property in the Gironde catches their eye. It ticks all the boxes : price, location, setting, style, potential and accessibility... the promised land. We manage to schedule two days at the end of the month for the three of us to view it. The seventeenth-century charterhouse in Graves wine-producing country is an authentic product of the region. It adjoins several dozen hectares of vineyards although it had lost the cultivation rights to them in a previous life. Nevertheless, there's still a beautiful French garden circling the buildings which Philippe loves; Giulia, who is concerned about the upkeep, a little less. On the other hand, they're both thrilled by the interiors which are laid out all on one level and run the full length of the house. The return trip to Paris is tiring. On top of the 750 km drive, I have to be prepared to answer their questions and work out where we go from here. We arrange to meet the following week to discuss matters with a clear head.

The dream like view of the vineyards receding into the distance announces the start of season 3. Giulia had under estimated her deep-rooted emotional attachment to her daughters and grandchildren with whom she's in almost daily contact. The prospect of seeing less of them is a truly painful one. In fact, making that kind of choice is actually unthinkable for her. Imagining herself in that situation had made her realise what a wrench it would be. Jean-Luc, who is less sensitive to having the family nearby, is keeping a low profile. In truth, he no longer knows what to do. The dream of moving is fading. When it comes down to it, he too is rather upset. There's an awkward silence. In this somewhat gloomy atmosphere, I announce a change of course. All that's missing is the drum roll. "We need to make a correction to the letter of engagement. Instead of 'in the south-west' it should read '30 minutes from the manor'."

My enthusiasm is contagious but I'm well aware of how difficult this new challenge will be. Finding a property in the provinces becomes infinitely more complex when that search gravitates towards Paris but with a budget and requirements which remain unchanged. Buying a larger property than the manor with the proceeds from its sale is challenging when the search area needs to fall within 40 minutes of Paris. Jean-Luc's income will be reduced so it would be unreasonable to adjust the planned budgets other than marginally. But I'm not prepared to throw in the towel without trying, so I carry on. Giulia and Jean-Luc have trouble believing it. They've known their chateau-owning neighbours for decades so, my goodness, they would know if a house was up for sale round here! I'm well positioned to know that there's a confidential market for this type of property. The search would be particularly sensitive and difficult and I also need to reassure Agnès and Philippe in Paris who continue to voice their impatience on a regular basis.

I have the advantage of knowing the region like the back of my hand. I pore over maps like a geographer. I list all the chateaux in the area and, believe me, there are many. 34 are listed in the historical monuments' archives. I found more than 59. The three computer screens in my office are transformed into a virtual battleground complete with star-studded maps. My search is colour-coded. Yellow dots mark the highest-rated chateaux, white the "second tier"; green dots are estates with more than 2 hectares of land, the type of property I'm looking for etc. You'll appreciate that green and yellow is a potentially winning combination. It's pains taking work but well worth the effort as I know it will serve me again and again.

Summer has passed and it's back to school. My searches have not been in vain. After months of compiling meticulous lists, my database identifies the owners of two chateaux which meet my criteria. By then it's late September and Agnès and Philippe have already been waiting patiently since mid-February... Giulia and Jean-Luc aren't particularly involved in the search; they're simply not convinced.

The first property to be thrown up by my search is located to the south of Senlis. It belongs to a business man who lives abroad. Trying to get hold of him is extraordinarily difficult. It takes me two weeks and three visits to the caretaker to gain his trust. He puts off getting back to me on rather vague pretexts. At the third attempt, I take a (male) colleague along with me. I finally get an answer scribbled on a piece of paper; an address in Paris. No name, just three initials and an address. Nicely played, sir! Although I'm grateful to him, I'm in no mood to embark on a wild goose chase or quibble over the matter any further and we take our leave. In fact, the initials belong to a company and I manage to get an appointment on the Champs Elysées with the chateau owner's private secretary. The secretary politely informs me that her employer is a very busy CEO of a CAC 40 company and, what's more, he lives mostly in the States. He's left very clear instructions to discourage anyone from approaching his chateau. I finally manage to meet him. He's polite but strongly opposed to the idea of selling his property, uninhabited though it is -apart from the zealous caretaker.

Approaching the second target is a little easier as the owner lives on site. Access to the property is set back from the road. A sports complex completely hides the boundary of what must once have been the grand driveway. The land had probably been bought by investors to fund the upkeep of the chateau. Fortunately, the proximity of the complex doesn't detract from the setting as the house is completely shielded by its wooded parkland. I look for the entrance which nowadays is through an imposing wrought iron gate at the opposite end from where you might expect, which gives me the opportunity to walk round the parkland and discover the ruins of the moat, probably the remains of an older chateau.

This time, I get in touch with the current owner using more traditional means. Letters and telephone calls eventually establish contact with the owner's daughter and it's Armelle who shows me round during my first visit in early November. She's in love with her family home. She recently got married and would love to buy out her brothers and sisters if she wasn't so disheartened by all the family squabbles of the last twenty years.

During the visit she tells me about the alterations and renovations carried out with such passion by her father. As she talks, you can almost see the story of her life since childhood unfolding in her eyes. The two main projects were the restoration of the stonework and the external pointing, including the onsite construction of cross mullions, and electricity which the head of the family had fully installed within the walls of the 850 m^2 living space. The completed renovations meant that the family could occupy more than half of the chateau in comfort. The corner pavilions and the second storey could potentially be used to set up a business, a small boutique hotel for example. There's reason to believe that the Princess of Harcourt, who purchased the county in 1702, demanded that the house be converted to form one of her residences. To the south, the rectangular main structure with its central pediment provides two levels of living space with cross-mullioned windows and slate

Mansart roofs with dormers. At right angles to each side of the central structure, two projections are supported by connecting square towers, two corner pavilions with lovely rounded shed dormers. To the north, there's a classical renaissance facade crowned with a triangular pediment and embellished with two round towers topped with elegant slate pepperpots. Inside, there was no mistaking the desire to reproduce the splendours of days gone by. Stone floors forming a checkerboard of black and white pebbles or, better still, marble with coloured geometric patterns and ceilings embellished with mouldings and gilded roses. Everything has been done to evoke eighteenth-century grandeur. On climbing the grand stone staircase, there's the chinoiserie-style washroom followed by the walk through the row of salons. It's easy to imagine how it must have felt to be an intimate of the Princess of Harcourt, especially on entering the crowning glory of the great gallery.

Obviously, I appreciate that Armelle, who grew up here under the caring influence of her father, feels sentimental about this place. When she describes the changes the house has undergone, she's revisiting her childhood. I can also see that the family conflicts are painful for her. It's a sensitive issue because, as she speaks, I begin to understand that her father is not actually the owner. The elderly gentleman is what's known as a "usufructuary" meaning he has a legal right to use the property although it belongs to someone else. I therefore need to get a better understanding of the situation. It's a delicate subject. Despite choosing my words carefully and being as gentle as I can, Armelle avoids my questions and falls silent. I ask her about her memories, trying to get at least some understanding of who the unknown players are. The mere mention of their name is almost taboo and but it seems they are the ones I'll have to deal with. It's another wild goose chase, with me once more in the role of detective and, to some extent, ethnologist as, if we're to envisage any future negotiations, I have no alternative other than to restore old connections, rights and influences as I make my discoveries, particularly from my dealings with the four family solicitors. After countless twists and turns, I'm determined to present Giulia and Jean-Luc with a case that leaves no loose ends. At this point, I know that ownership is shared among the three children and their mother, with whom Armelle and her father are not on speaking terms.

The three winter months are useful for gaining the trust of the key players. Each member of the family, in their own corner of France, bears a grievance of varying degrees against the others. I listen actively, I respond, I objectivise, I put my interpersonal skills to the test and do my best to manage the social regulations. My goal is to persuade the 'wait and see'proponents to sell and for the vendors to offer the chateau to my clients. One by one, all the key players, spouses and advisors of each faction end up taking part in almost daily bilateral discussions : father, mother, daughter, son, son-in-law, partner, solicitors, bailiffs and other trusted friends of each party...

I assure them of my discretion and transparency. I position myself as the guarantor of impartiality and begin by arranging for the property to be valued by the Estates who'll determine its market value in its current state. This is a symbolic act which confirms my role as a neutral facilitator. It's also a means of avoiding a second valuation by another estate agent who would slow down or even manipulate the process for their own ends. (I detest the practice of artificially inflating prices to get a foot in the door.) Finally, to pre-empt the questions that were sure to arise, I invite a number of tradesmen from among my contacts to provide estimates for work to bring the property up to current standards - sanitation, electricity, heating etc. - and in particular to determine how much life is left in the roof, something that had been worrying me.

At last, everyone is in agreement and I can finally show the chateau to Giulia and Jean-Luc. But then, all of a sudden, time begins to speed up again. My mediation over several months has been so successful that the key players are now all in favour of selling up as quickly as possible with me as their agent... or perhaps not. It's unthinkable that a year's work could be stolen away in just a few days by some lucky Johnny-come-lately.

The chateau is under snow by mid-February which comes as a complete surprise to Giulia and Jean-Luc. I had managed the suspense right up to the last minute so that I could present the results of my work like a trophy. They fall in love with it immediately. There are three euphoric viewings as they get to know the property and the offer comes in at the asking price. It's quickly accepted. Both exchanges of contract are signed in the same week in mid-March just before my birthday, one at the manor, the other at the chateau. In June, Agnès and Philippe and Giulia and Jean-Luc sign their deeds of sale on the same day in their respective solicitor's offices. Were the two deals linked - or not at all? That is the question. The die is cast! The fourth season can begin.

Flemish blue

"Potverdekke! It's not Europe, it's Eutrope! You're not 'Brusselese', are you?" Paulus laughs heartily. "This is Saintonge!" He's referring to Eutrope, Saint Eutrope, the evangelist from the old Saintonge province. His legend dates back to the first century. Sent by Pope Clement, he came from Greece to evangelise the Santons and is said to have converted Eustelle, the daughter of the Roman governor. Kim exclaims that Santon figurines come from Provence. Paulus laughs even harder, contradicts her and explains that the Santons were the Gallic tribe which founded the town of Saintes and the province of Saintonge and that it has nothing to do with the fact that 'santoun' in the Provence dialect means 'little saints'.

"Stop showing off, Paulus," jokes Kim, a little put out. Paulus Rijkaard is a former client of mine. I found him his dream home in Saint Jean d'Angely where he has invited me today to introduce me to Kim and Hendrik. Paulus and Antje have something of a 'boontje' (literally a 'little bean') for their new home. You might say they've got a bit of a crush on it... "We knew what a beautiful part of the country it was so when Hélène showed us this house we went for it 'volle petrol'", says Paulus. He explains that his friends Hendrik and Kim are looking for somewhere sunny but, like them, they don't enjoy really hot weather and it would be lovely for them all if they could be neighbours.
So he'd invited us all to 'babel' about their plans. We have a chat. Hendrik doesn't say much before handing over to his wife who will be my point of contact. It's all up to her. In any case, he spends his

life taking flights and doing business. It's pretty straight forward. He wants 'an old-fashioned cottage as a second home' with (he counts off the points on his fingers) 1. Sun 2. A mild climate 3. Peace and calm 4. Sea views and 5. Leisure activities for the family. "Other than that, you have carte blanche as long as Kim approves." A dream comes true! It must have been obvious from my expression and Paulus says their 'whiskers are curling' and that we should 'take a pot', which means they hope the project will be successful and we're going to drink to that!

Now it's over to Kim. I can see that she's already fully committed to the project and has lots of ideas, perhaps rather too many. I ask her how her house in Antwerp is decorated. She adores 'shabby chic', the trendy style which consists of creating elegant, new furnishings from old, worn ones. One particular word keeps cropping up : light. They need light, they want sunshine, the rooms must be bright and there must be lots of big windows. I note it all down. I already have some ideas but I play for time. I'll come up with some suggestions to narrow down the search. When are they coming back? "No idea," replies Kim. Hendrik is always at 'Macapette', she says (meaning miles from nowhere) and she's usually stuck at home on her own with the children.

Three weeks later Kim answers my Skype call. I can see part of her living room on my screen. It is indeed chic, cosy and bright. "It's retro", she says. She smiles and concedes, somewhat grudgingly", and perhaps a touch kitsch". I tell her where I am with my investigations. As instructed, I went in search of sea and sun and would recommend the area around La Rochelle : an exceptional amount of sunshine (as much as the Côte d'Azur making it the sunniest place on the Atlantic coast without the hot weather thanks to the sea breeze) ; lots of leisure activities including sailing ; the nearby islands of Ré, Oléron, Aix and Madame; the beautiful old town and the 'Porte Océane' quarter, all dating from the twelfth century with a rich historical and urban heritage. And their friends, the Rijkaards, only an hour's drive away. To fit the bill perfectly, there must be peace and quiet and a sea view. With all these criteria in mind I'd selected a manor, a traditional Charente-style house and a contemporary home. It's not easy to find an old house in a peaceful spot on the coast. And if you do, they're not always very bright. The third house doesn't have the period character but it does have large windows overlooking the sea. "These are the three options. I'll email you the links to the videos and you can call me back when you've watched them." "Great!" says Kim and she hangs up.

I get a Skype call twenty minutes later. Kim gets straight to the point. The manor house is poncey, the traditional Charente-style house is nice but can I find them something brighter, the sea view from the contemporary house is 'tchiniss' (meaning downmarket). I recap what she'd said to be sure I'd understood. I explain that we could expand the search area but at the risk of losing out on an excellent location for their holiday home. So they would sacrifice their requirement for an old house if they found one that had character, great views and light. I hang up but the last webcam image of Kim remains fixed in my mind. You don't need an eighteenth-century pediment to celebrate shabby chic ! Let's prioritise the sea view and I'll give some thought as to how we can introduce character and light.

Located on the harbour, open views over the Isle of Ré, a 5,000 m² plot, a spacious living room overlooking the sea, open-plan fitted kitchen, master bedroom with en suite, four bedrooms each with their own bathroom, an office, art studio, patio... Not bad. I love the large bay windows and the view is superb. But this big square house doesn't offer much scope for creativity. What about this secluded villa? A classic example of a 1970s build with no character whatsoever. But it overlooks the dunes and has great views. It's quiet and peaceful. I think I'll take a look.

I call Kim on Skype. The children are in bed by this time. I explain why I'm calling and show her my own photos using another screen. The ones taken by the owner don't give much away. These houses are coming back into fashion as long as they're skilfully renovated. I describe the house, I make suggestions and get a bit carried away... I'd spotted a place selling original building materials close by... the bay windows could go in such and such a place... Kim finally gets interested. Half an hour later she confesses that she'd had a quick cigarette - she was a little scared - and thought I didn't 'have all my chips in the same bag'. She's now almost convinced and wants to see the property for herself.

Hendrik trusts her judgement so Kim comes on her own. The children are staying with her sister. I pick her up at La Rochelle airport which has direct flights to Brussels, an hour's drive from Antwerp. It's an important factor. She says she's delighted to get away, it's a welcome break from the daily routine but five kilometres further down the road she admits she's still scared stiff. She mustn't lose the plot over the crazy idea of buying a house in France. "Is it far?" she asks. It's true, she does seem a bit stressed. "But", she adds as if to reassure herself, "you seem to have your head screwed on". I smile. The viewing took some time as, in our minds, we were redesigning each room, decorating it with wooden cladding and giving it structure with old, wood stained beams. Some of the walls are knocked through, windows are put in and patio doors are visualised in the bay windows. We redesign the outside walls; what about a patio? Kim is over the moon. She's up for the challenge and asks me to find her a good architect and decorator, skilled and trustworthy artisans.

My PC heats up during our Skype chat. It's been six months since the project began and Kim and Hendrik are the proud owners of the former 70s villa which now looks more like a loft. Even though it's still a little rough around the edges, it already has lots of character with its bright, split-level spaces overlooking the dunes and the azure sea. The structural work is complete and the shabby chic operation is about to begin. Kim is very careful in her choice of designer and asks what I think of the different shades of blue in the Farrow & Ball range of paints. A comical misunderstanding ensues. Oops ! It's just the webcam distorting the colours. Hendrik comes to the screen. He says hello and, all smiles, tells me I've become Kim's Jiminy Cricket, which she doesn't find at all amusing. "That's him trying to be funny again", she complains. But Hendrik adds seriously: "You know, we really are completely blue about this house!"

P.S. Paulus later explained that he meant head over heels…

Dionysus and Apollo

The main house dates back to the late eighteenth century and the adjoining buildings to the one after that, a total of 400 square metres to be restored. I'm showing Wanda round the twenty rooms. She says nothing and I don't break the silence. She's getting a feel of the place. This is the first time I've been to a viewing with her but I think I know her rather well. We've talked and corresponded such a lot. We've been walking round the buildings for some time now. She asks for a technical opinion on the work required. She wants to know if the structure is sound, the timber frame in particular. To my mind, there's only finishing work to be done. I give her the estimate. She's reassured. In any case, a professional builder will be conducting a formal assessment. We return to the wine storehouse where we'd started the viewing. The layout of the storehouse might be a deal-breaker. It's the centrepiece of the project. Set opposite the main house, it's a large rectangular building of almost 300 square metres. A paved courtyard separates them. With the two adjoining buildings at right angles, the courtyard is almost square. It could have had something of a military feel but with its resplendent lime trees it's simply majestic. The storehouse has the potential for a huge loft ; the possibilities are endless but for now there's not much to see other than rough stone and beams. Once we're through the huge doorway, Wanda stops short and appears to be thinking, staring into the void. Then she does an about-turn and rushes back outside.

We return to the other side of the storehouse facing the hectare of parkland and the lake. In the background a leafy forest flows over limestone slopes; you can just tell the oaks from the rustic maples. On both sides of the pond, wooded islands dot the vineyards like moments of silence between the expanses of fruit. Behind the vines, at the foot of the hills, the distant river winds its way through the arbour. You can almost hear the silence rustling in the leaves. I turn and softly explain to Wanda that here, between the beams, is where the storehouse should be opened up and the windows installed. She agrees and looks away again to admire the natural beauty of the place. The storehouse is slightly elevated and the gently undulating valleys of vineyards and woodland stretch out before our eyes towards the forest foothills like an ode to nature. From the wooded grove on our left, a tree-lined archway beckons us to set off again through the rows of trained vines. Wanda seems happy. I think we understand each other. Once again, like many times over the last year, our minds are coming together in quiet communion. She's been seeking a temple of musical creativity, a place to inspire artistic expression and one which will be both open and secure. I think we're nearing that goal. Wanda must have read my thoughts as she adds, "a temple of extremes, of excess and harmony, a temple to Dionysus, the god of wine and ecstasy and Apollo, the bringer of poetry and music."

She goes back into the storehouse. "Yes, you're absolutely right. The picture windows between the beams will create a fantastic view over this theatre of green," she says. She chooses her words with care. In this theatre the recording studio will occupy the dress circle with the vineyards and pond in the orchestra pit and the forest taking centre stage. From a technical point of view, I'm sure it's feasible. The architect will confirm. No doubt he'll also have some original suggestions to make. We'll need to convene all the members of the acoustic design team so that everyone has an understanding of the needs of the others : the size and location of the studio, the control room, the voice recording booths and so on. Given the dimensions, several different configurations could be envisaged. Should there be another auditorium or should there be more chill-out rooms? It's not the same for the equipment suppliers. The outer shell has no bearing on the choice of technical options. In any case, a sound engineer, a friend of Wanda's, will also be attending the project meeting. Wanda's head must be in a spin. I suppose she's able to focus her thoughts but, with her involvement in so many activities and projects, the various options must all be jostling for her attention.

As a famous composer and multi-instrumentalist, she has a wealth of experience in musical direction, arranging and performance and has lost count of her successes collaborating with great artists in musicals, films and television. And now she's turning her hand to musical production. A property project is always linked to a life project but the connection can make itself felt to varying degrees. For Wanda, this move is critical. The location first of all, a place to live, to spend time with family, a place for her to create and for all the artists she hopes to attract there. Just a short distance from Bordeaux, the chosen spot combines accessibility with the tranquillity of rural life. A former wine estate, the vineyard was sold to the neighbouring chateaux which means the old winery is surrounded by pleasant countryside without the hard work that goes with it. The artistic dimension is important of course. First of all, the right vibration. A joyful noise, a poetic chord, the murmur of ripe grapes and rustling leaves, the ripple of a heron on the still surface of the pond. The storehouse is composed of the riches of the land. An energising return to source to participate in a celebration of creativity. Then there's the strength that comes from a meeting of minds, the mighty power of collective emotion. The storehouse, like an alchemist's laboratory, will ferment the flow of thought and distil the essence of immortality. The many rooms in the surrounding buildings will welcome the atoms at rest until that moment when they come together in a chain reaction.

As a one-woman band, Wanda needs to set every aspect of the project to music and their respective costs are worrying her. Is she's to carry out the renovation work on the storehouse, she needs to get the property at the best possible price. That's perfectly reasonable. I did in fact recommend that course of action as I feel the asking price is too high. I have a fair price in mind for both parties, which I've agreed with Wanda as a target, with a well-crafted argument based on comparable recent sales in the area. This negotiation is my final, key responsibility. A meeting is organised with the joint owners who've decided not to appoint a representative. Everyone wants to be directly involved in the negotiations and hear my arguments in person which doesn't make my task any easier.

The evening before the meeting, tragedy strikes. It's late when Wanda calls me in a distressed state. Her father, a shareholder in the company which was due to finance the purchase of the property, has come out against the project, at least in its current form. He thinks the choice of infrastructure is too ambitious and that it's too far from town. Wanda explains that she's tried to win him round but to no avail. Her banker, accountant, spouse and friends are all adamant : the salvation of the project depends on daddy's cash. Wanda is devastated. It's a disaster! Her father isn't exempt from the laws of the universe, I murmur. Today his world is dominated by the reasoned influence of Apollo. I suggest awakening his slumbering Dionysus with an invitation to visit the future temple of music. The date is set. On the big day, her father arrives all smiles. It only took him half an hour to get here, which is promising. He wouldn't have thought so. You already know what happens next. There's no need to repeat it. If you've forgotten, go back to the second paragraph. The magic of the place does its work as Wanda talks him through her plans. Her father is thrilled, his daughter is decidedly a genius... and the meeting with the vendors is back on the agenda.

Apollo's steady cadence will work its magic. In the words of Hesiod, 'For it is through the Muses and far-shooting Apollo that there are singers upon the earth and players upon the lyre'.

Roots

"Good morning. This is Maître Verneuil of the legal firm, ST International Partner. Antoine M... recommended I get in touch with you. I have an American client who wishes to invest in France. Something special, you understand..." The intermediary explains in a somewhat convoluted manner that it's a huge undertaking. I appreciate that but I'd like to know exactly what kind of 'special' we're talking about. "It's historical... my client wants to trace his roots. Of course that requires investigation. But before providing you with any further details, we'd like to know if this is something you would be interested in taking on and, if so, how you would propose to proceed." In fact, the corporate lawyer wants to know how capable I would be of completing the assignment and if any preconditions would be required. I explain that, if necessary, I'll be able to call on the appropriate specialists.

These Americans don't waste any time, which I find refreshing. Frank Taylory calls me from Los Angeles the next day. He's delighted with the way I responded to Maître Verneuil's call and congratulates me on having accepted the assignment. It's not a style of communication we're used to in France. Frank is Mr. Marlowe's assistant. I'm informed that John B. Marlowe is very busy with his business interests and that Frank has been tasked with briefing me so that I can present them with my plan of action and terms in a few days' time. I'm tempted to tell him that would be 'awesome'. Mr. Marlowe is passionate about history and genealogy. He has French ancestors so he has strong emotional ties to France and visits regularly for both business and pleasure. He had therefore come up with the idea of combining the two and investing in a property in France. More specifically, he'd like to buy something with a connection to his ancestors. It goes without saying that this property should be steeped in history and reflect his French heritage but also be within a stone's throw of an international airport. He'll also need a helipad. The house will have to accommodate four or five families with children, all at the same time, and there must be opportunities for tourist and leisure activities nearby. "There's no price limit but you'll need to put forward solid arguments in favour of the properties you select. The same applies to estimates for any renovation work you might recommend. There's no set deadline but if you're able to act quickly, you'll be remunerated accordingly. Do you have any questions?" I smile at my phone. It was such a monotonous speech, it could have been mistaken for a military operation order. That's probably why the newspaper, *Sud-Ouest*, had dubbed me 'the James Bond of real estate'."Yes, I have a question. I'll need details of what's known of the family's history!" "I'm emailing you the file right now. Can you confirm receipt?" Frank is very professional. Okay, I'll give it some thought but I can already say that one of my conditions would be to have access to Mr Marlowe. It's much more than just a financial investment for him. These businessmen are naturally sparing with their time but they need to understand that digging for your roots isn't like digging for oil. You don't want to run out of gas.

The antivirus flags up a spam email. It's from an American company and is signed by Frank Taylory. I open up the protected files. Luckily it's Saturday evening and I can spend some time reading Marlowe's copious documents. It turns out to be an impenetrable list of dates and events. It would have been worse if his French origins had gone back as far as Columbus! Yes, that is possible. Did you know that one of his sailors was French, a man by the name of Cousin? He joined the great seafarer on his famous expedition of 1492, furious at having been dismissed for insubordination when he returned to Dieppe. But what's really astonishing is that he'd already sailed to America on a previous voyage in 1488, four years before its official discovery.

Marlowe's first French ancestor was a trapper, Jacques Marquet, who travelled around between the Appalachian and Rocky Mountains in the early seventeenth century. He then went on to settle in New France, the first permanent French colony founded by Samuel de Champlain of Sainton, originally in Port Royal and then in Quebec. He had apparently befriended the American Indians and had even married one of their daughters. According to a tradition passed down through the family, he traded in beaver fur which was worn by elegant Europeans on their top hats or jacket collars. Jacques Marquet had two sons. The eldest, Sicaire, accompanied Robert Cavelier de la Salle on his expedition on the River Colbert, later renamed the Mississippi. La Salle enjoyed the favour of Colbert, who had taken over from Richelieu in encouraging the development of New France. He initially occupied the island of Montreal and organised expeditions around the lakes of Ontario and Erie. In 1681, he navigated the Mississippi through Indian territory to the Gulf of Mexico and, in the name of Louis XIV, King of France and Navarre, Louisiana was born...

At around the same time, two thousand French Huguenots, driven out by the revocation of the Edict of Nantes in 1685, settled in ports such as Boston and New York, since many of them were traders, and in the colonies, particularly in South Carolina. They were quickly integrated into British circles and married into the local elite except for Margaret Bury who married the merchant, Charles Marquet, Sicaire's younger brother who had perhaps found another outlet for his furs in New Amsterdam, the future New York. Margaret was the daughter of Huguenots who had taken refuge on the island of Manhattan which the Dutch Governor had bought from the Indians. They had come to the promised land after a stay in the United Provinces of the Netherlands where they had anglicised their names. An accident of history meant that the marriage of Charles and Margaret was held in the village of Staten Island, opposite Brooklyn. Today, these two boroughs are linked by the Verrazano-Narrows suspension bridge named in honour of the explorer, Giovanni da Verrazano. Sent by François 1st of France, he was the first European to set foot on the site of present-day New York, which he named New Angoulême. I found out later that Jacques Marquet, the father of the groom, was in fact born in Angoulême. Charles and Margaret Marquet had five children.

Another branch of John B. Marlowe's descendants includes a representative of the wave of French immigration which took place in 1815 in the wake of the Napoleonic wars. It was in Texas in unknown circumstances that Kate Smith met and married Imperial Colonel Maury, a widower since the death of his first wife, Jeanne deMontignac. Maury was then among 150 officers who joined GeneralsLallemand and Rigaud in establishing a colony, Champ d'Asile, on the banks of the Trinity River. But the young, impetuous colonel, who had been awarded the Legion of Honour cross at Austerlitz, swiftly fled the famine and disease with his wife and his gold. He joined the French community in Louisiana, where, with the support of his wife's family, he made his fortune in cotton.

So that gives me three leads to explore : Jacques Marquet and Margaret Bury in the seventeenth century and Colonel Maury in the nineteenth. I start by digging through the archive material Frank Taylory had sent me. I have a comprehensive collection of slides containing details of parish registers and records of birth, marriages and deaths with the added bonus of a few administrative declarations. Most of them are French. With the growth of the Internet, many of our government departments have made their digital archives available online but it's not always easy to decipher entries made with a quill pen, especially if the ink has faded over the years.

A Rochefort priest writes in his register of 1702 that he had baptised one Jacques Marquet, born in Angoulême, the son of Sicaire and Jeanne Marquet. A year before, the same parish records the marriage of a Sicaire Marquet, tailor in Rochefort and Jeanne, daughter of a weaver in the same town. Presumably they're the same people and it's notable that Jacques Marquet's eldest son has his grandfather's name, Sicaire. It's not a particularly promising lead as the Rochefort region isn't exactly famous for its international transport links. You could certainly imagine the affluent John B. Marlowe travelling by private jet or helicopter but I mustn't indulge in wishful thinking and need to force myself to follow the instructions I'd been given. After all, Frank had specified, 'close to an international airport'.

But Jacques Marquet doesn't disappear from the story completely as his youngest son, Charles, married Margaret Bury whose story I now investigate. Marlowe was very lucky in that the young settler kept a diary which was passed down through successive generations. It also provided him with information on Margaret's in-laws. The young woman had in fact anglicised her name. Prior to her stay in the Netherlands, she had been Marguerite Burie. She came from a family of Guyenne merchants who had advanced socially through the purchase of royal grants. Her ancestors, nobles of Fentenac, had acquired this fiefdom and continued to invest in vineyards and mills. Through marriage they had also been able to incorporate land into their family estates and property from the maternal line can be found in the region of Saint-Emilion. So, with that, we have a few topographical discoveries which tick all the boxes, just an hour's drive from Bordeaux-Merignac airport.

Colonel Maury was born in the reign of Louis XVI in Bergerac, the son of a notary. Information about the family is fairly scarce despite the existence (following the French Revolution) of a register of births, marriages and deaths at the time of his first marriage and the social standing of the Maury family. Perhaps there would be more information available about the notary, Maury of Bergerac. For now, I suspend my research into Jeanne de Montignac, first wife of the imperial officer. These were probably the Dordogne Montignacs, going by the marriage certificate. Also, if there's one lead to explore as a priority, it should be Bergerac as its small airport has more traffic than the one at Brive-la-Gaillarde, even if it means travelling via London.

Common sense would have my search start in Guyenne where there's actual evidence of family history and a promising search area. I explain all this in a long email to Frank Taylory, adding my conditions and a few reservations. I don't have long to wait for an answer, which is as friendly as it is brief, along the lines of, "Yes to everything, there's no need to call." Los Angeles really is the Wild West! Guyenne, however, is rather less exotic. It doesn't take me long to list the surnames of the descendants of Marguerite Burie Fentenac, aka Margaret Bury of New York. Websites on local history and Guyenne heraldry in particular make my task much easier. By cross-referencing my research with specialist publications, I draw up a list of the family's properties and prioritise the ones which have, or may have, more than fifteen bedrooms. I want to produce an initial inventory and, once I've incorporated information from my partners and sifted through the field research, I'll draw up a list of potential properties.

Most of the properties I'd pre-selected were not for sale. I'd had high hopes of renovating a lovely abandoned hamlet whose central building had attractive Renaissance features but the town hall informed me that my plans for its development would not be possible. I now only have two cards to play, including a joker which I was keeping up my sleeve : a neoclassical chateau which complies with most of the practical specifications I'd been given. The body of the main building is rectangular and flanked by two pavilions in a raised position lending a majestic feel to the whole house. The horizontal lines are highlighted by the use of cornices, listels and window lintels on the entire facade. The price is completely unreasonable given the state of the roof. Everything is negotiable, you might say. But what's bothering me most is that Margaret emigrated to America in the seventeenth century and this is a nineteenth-century house ! I can't see myself explaining to John Marlowe that it's a chateau which belonged to the descendants of his ancestors. He would look at me in bewilderment as he chewed on his big cigar, bemoaning the fact that, for Margaret, that would be a kind of Back to the Future...

Last but not least, the chateau of... was originally a country house set in the middle of a wine estate. Although most of the land was sold off to neighbouring farmers, the building remained in the Burie de Fentenac family for more than four centuries. The construction of this former country retreat was begun by Margaret's great-grandfather in 1565. Major alterations were carried out in the seventeenth century so it's highly likely that Margaret would have been familiar with most of the current layout. It's made up of a main building with a perpendicular wing and a polygonal stair turret in the angle. The slate roof has dormers with triangular pediments. The floor above the reception rooms has only nine bedrooms but a similar number could be created in the attic space. The property also has a large number of outbuildings which could be renovated: orangeries, wine storehouses, a dovecot, outhouses and so on. In total, I estimate there's potential for over twenty-five rooms excluding the reception spaces. It's a fabulous discovery in a tourist area, 45 minutes from Bordeaux, in the middle of the great wine estates and the price seems to be negotiable. I think it might be time to contact Frank and get access to the big boss.

I'm waiting for him in the arrivals hall at Bordeaux-Merignac airport. A dynamic, young, forty-something, dressed in a loose shirt and jeans and chewing gum walks past me and makes a quarter turn. He doesn't ask me the time. He introduces himself. John Marlowe. I look around for his entourage. No Barbie-doll secretary, no quadrilingual assistant. A bilingual speaker is waiting for us at the chateau and I now wonder if his services will actually be required. But any doubts on that score quickly fade when John B. Marlowe puts his hands in his jeans pockets, leans back and hollers, "Well done! C'est cool."

Eugénie

- When can you come?
- Now, if that suits. I'm not far away.
- Yes, that's fine. I'll see you shortly.

It's an elderly gentleman who opens the door to me, one who's already well into old age although his voice had sounded young on the phone. He's charming, with old-fashioned manners to match the sophisticated interior of his home. The house is a *'meulière'*, a period property, half-manor, half-villa, a common design in this stylish part of the Ile-de-France. We're to have tea in front of the French window which opens onto the garden. The silverware is gleaming. He must have people to do for him. Monsieur definitely isn't the sort to polish it himself. In true gentlemanly fashion, he shows me round, displaying a combination of consideration and gallantry. I love the galleries with the wooden, spindled bannisters at the top of the stairs on each floor. The climb is quite strenuous and I'm almost out of breath.

Some of his acquaintances had told him about me. He trusts me. He's keen to make that clear. "Trust is critical, you see". I'm trying to understand the situation but Monsieur, with a level of intrigue worthy of the royal court, remains enigmatic until he invites me to take a seat on the red damask Napoleon III sofa (blackened pear wood, apparently). He has a plan he'd like to talk to me about. Whether he's keeping up the suspense as some sort of literary device or is burdened by an outmoded sense of decorum, I can't say.

Having taken the long way round, we finally get to the point : he's 'met someone'. Against all odds, the vagaries of fortune are once again urging him to action. He never did know how to take his time. A wonderful opportunity has presented itself to him and he's already taken far too long to act. Her name is Eugénie and he isn't going to procrastinate any further, not for an empire. I'm to be responsible for everything : the sale of this property, the search for the new one, the viewings and the negotiation. He's no longer of an age to put himself under pressure. These days he delegates. Be that as it may, he wasn't made for these times : he doesn't have a computer or a mobile phone. He works around it? No, he insists on it. He is, however, of an age for smoked tea and strolls on the promenade at sunset. Other than that, he doesn't mind. The 'haggling' will be down to me, that's my responsibility. He has no children and no-one to be accountable to. He does, nonetheless, expect me to be accountable to him. "I'm counting on your ability to be succinct", he quips pleasantly. "Full speed ahead!" he proclaims with gusto. "You've got a name that's predestined for that. And all these things" (he gestures to the silver teapot and stylish furniture) "have no importance whatsoever." He's going to sell everything and find a little house with a small garden by the sea, a mild climate, in town, with all amenities, a stone's throw from the sea...

"This is my last bachelor home; we can't afford to get it wrong," he says. We discuss the search area. He's thinking about Aquitaine. His beloved Eugénie knows people there. Arcachon, for example. He's always liked it and Bordeaux isn't too far away. We consider a plan B and move down the coast on the map, fingers pointing toward the south. Biscarosse, Mimizan. No, too small. We settle on Biarritz and Saint-Jean-de-Luz. But, remember, the town centre and amenities must be within walking distance but no late-night bars or other annoyances. A house, but no specifics. I ask why as, in my opinion, an apartment would be more practical at his age. I can see him in a nice apartment with a balcony. No, he's set on a house. Not necessarily an Arcachon-style house, although, granted, that's traditional, but a villa would be more convenient and comfortable. We'll have to see. Yes, a small garden with a patio, somewhere to have coffee amidst the flowers, but a garden, not a country estate. No upkeep. Secateurs and, at worst, a bit of grass for the gardener to deal with.A luxury villa.No need for much space. A bedroom for her and one for him. An office-cum-library is important. They must be able to read quietly in natural light, light that's coming from the left of the office. He doesn't much like kitchens. So-called American kitchens are just trendy foolishness and not for him. Don't mix apples and oranges. He can't stand the sound of pots and pans. A living room-dining room or two separate rooms, it doesn't matter. So that makes five rooms in total, let's say 120 square metres minimum, shall we ? 150-200 would be more reasonable. Well, that'll depend on the market. It would be great if everything was on one level but perhaps that's asking too much. Ah yes, cupboards. He wants cupboards. Lots of them. They should be all over the house or, if not, you can 'find me a joiner and he can sort out the space... I don't want any big wardrobes cluttering up the place. It looks old-fashioned."

Driving on the motorway, I reflect fondly on this sprightly new client who's so enthralled by his romance. "I want everything white, bright, chic, modern. My fiancée doesn't like the stuffy bourgeois look but it still needs to be stylish." The satnav has come up with some nonsensical route again but I've no time to correct it as my phone is ringing on the dashboard. And it is he, the fiancé. "I just wanted to say, dear lady, that there's no need to rule out properties which require renovation as long as the work is carried out quickly." Functionality and aesthetics are to be the priority. That had indeed been my understanding and he wasn't to worry. He hangs up after some pleasantries that sound sincere. It's late and I'm tired. Unusually for me, I put off starting work on the search till the next day.

I'm putting the final touches to my battle plan and am just about to dig out some old files when the phone rings. "My dear lady, it's a real pleasure to speak to you again on this beautiful sunny day. Is it as lovely where you are?" Monsieur had spent the evening with his fiancée. She's delighted with the plan and ideally wants to look for something in the Basque Country. Her wishes are his command. Since this is a love story, I suggest not ruling out any love-at-first-sight properties that might come along. I know from experience that it's important not to become a prisoner of your preconceived notions. Homes are affairs of the heart. You might find that rather obscure; I don't. When it comes to emotions, motivations are complex. He agrees with me, reproaches himself for his childish impatience and promises not to trouble me again. Nevertheless, he calls the next day to ask me how we're going to manage as he doesn't use a computer 'like other people do'. In fact, he doesn't use one at all. I remind him I'd promised to come and see him in a month's time. Oh, yes, he'd forgotten but that's absolutely fine. I'm looking for a house on one level but am still convinced that a nice apartment would suit him better. I'd seen one with a magnificent sea view and a balcony. I locate a few houses in Biarritz and Saint-Jean-de-Luz, none of which are quite right or which aren't within the budget I've been given to work with. I think Biarritz isa better choice as it has the amenities I'd been asked for. Monsieur calls me. He's given it some thought and thinks Biarritz would be suitable. I agree; my thoughts exactly.

My visit to Paris is eventful. Out of the blue along-time client asks me to find him a house, half-manor, half-villa, 30 minutes from Paris. I might just have the solution... In fact, I'm off to visit my future Basque couple. Madame is there too and she's just as sprightly as her fiancé. I tell them about my search and put forward the idea of an attractive apartment with a balcony. In fact, they'd been thinking along those very lines. This might be the one... I turn on the computer... suspense... and there you have it! Biarritz town centre, beaches and shops within walking distance, a beautiful Art Deco apartment, 160 square metres, on the top floor with a balcony and a lift, spacious reception rooms, 3 bedrooms and 2 bathrooms... I suggest they don't waste any time. They're prepared to travel down to see it but they're worried. The words tumble out : funds, banker, bridging loan and so on. Happily, I'm in a position to reassure them. I have other good news : a viewer for this house. One phone call later the appointment is made for that same evening. Two phone calls later the viewing of the Biarritz apartment is arranged for the day after next. Three phone calls later the hotel is booked. The next day the three of us drive down in my car. The new couple look at each other, speechless. They can't believe it. Neither can I. Sometimes twists of fate are simply incredible. The sale and the purchase are finalised three months later. "Eugénie in Biarritz," exclaims Monsieur as he signs the contract. "A royal homecoming indeed!"

Acknowledgements

I would particularly like to thank my husband without whom none of this would have been possible.

My thanks also to our four children, the fire in my hearth.

Finally, thank you to Lynne and Margaux for their commitment to this project.

      After graduating from business school, Hélène had completed an international business studies course in London when she was recruited by McCain to introduce their brand to France. She was responsible for one quarter of the French market before being head-hunted by Douwe Egberts.

10 house moves and 4 children later, she joined the Entrepreneurial Network where she caught the business-creation bug, setting up her own company in April 2008.

She opened her first agency in Chantilly where her personal approach was an immediate hit. Today, based in green and sunny South-West, she happily combines country family living with non-stop work. She now operates across the whole of France. An accomplished business woman, Hélène is constantly innovating to fulfil her dream of "renovating" the world of real estate to reflect the beauty of the properties she sells!

www.ingramcontent.com/pod-product-compliance
Lightning Source LLC
Chambersburg PA
CBHW070352130626
46556CB00007B/3150